GUIDE TO THE CHURCH
IN THE HOLY LAND

By
Geries Sa'ed Khoury

ISBN
965 — 232 — 009 — 9

AL-HAKEM PRINTING PRESS -NAZARETH

Tel. 065-54135

" *May they all be one.*
Father, may they be one in us,
as you are in me and I am in you,
so that the world may believe it was you who sent
me. "

John 17:21.

"When Pentecost day came round, they had all met in one room, when suddenly they heard what sounded like a powerful wind from heaven, the noise of which filled the entire house in which they were sitting; and something appeared to them that seemed like tongues of fire; these separated and came to rest on the head of them. They were all filled with the Holy Spirit, and began to speak foreign languages as the Spirit gave them the gift of speech." Acts, 2:1-4.

"The faithful all lived together and owned everything in common; they sold their goods and possessions and shared out the proceeds among themselves according to what each one needed.

They went as a body to the Temple every day but met in their houses for the breaking of bread; they shared their food gladly and generously; they praised God and were looked up to by everyone. Day by day the Lord added to their community those destined to be saved." Acts, 2:44-47.

FORWARD

We present our warm greetings and thanks for this book to our beloved son, Dr. Geries Sa'ed Khoury, Director of the "Christianity in the Holy Land" programme at the Ecumenical Institute of Tantur. It is the first of its kind to appear in the Holy Land. It is an informative introduction to the church of Jerusalem in the richness of its history, spirituality, culture and traditions. Dr. Geries Sa'ed Khoury did the work with great love for this church and with an admirable enthusiasm. His aim is to acquaint pilgrims with the Church in the Holy Land and its spiritual values.

We welcome the beloved pilgrims who come to visit the holy places, and assure them that the Church of Jerusalem and the Holy Land is worthy of their respect and love. This Church has borne witness to the richness and culture of the traditions and the value of the holy places for 2000 years, even through trials of martyrdom. The Christian communities of Jerusalem are ancient communities, going back to the Church of Pentecost as founded through the Apostles. The Church of Jerusalem is the Mother Church and in its name we welcome pilgrims and all those who love the church in the Holy Land. Congratulations! You are on a visit to your Mother! Our prayer for all pilgrims and readers of this book is that they may grow in faith, hope and love and remember that we are all sons of the Resurrection.

Greetings and good wishes to all from the Mother Church of Jerusalem, the Church of Pentecost, the Church of Resurrection!

4/4/1984   Archbishop Lutfi Laham
                                       Greek-Catholic Melkite
                                 Patriachal Vicar in Jerusalem.

PREFACE

It is hoped that this brief guide to the churches in the Holy Land will serve as a useful companion during your pilgrimage. The guide is not scholarly in intent but I hope that it will provide you with a clear outline of the history of the different churches in the Holy Land, their rites and customs.

It is also hoped that this booklet will encourage you to visit and pray in the different churches, to enter more fully into their spiritual traditions and to know more about their pastoral and social life.

I hope that your pilgrimage to the land where Jesus was born, lived and died will be blessed and safe and that you will grow faithfully in his love.

I would like to take this opportunity to thank the executive committee of «Jerusalem 84» who prompted and encouraged me to produce this work. Thanks are also due to my wife and family for encouraging me to write it:to Ghada Yousef Naffa',

Dona Harvey and Peter Stucky for their assistance. Special thanks are due to Stephen Need for many helpful comments during the preparation of the manuscript.

Furthermore, I am grateful to the Rector and Staff of Tantur and for the facilities there.

Finally, I am indebted to Bishop Lutfi Laham the Greek -Catholic Patriarchal Vicar in Jerusalem for reading and writing the forward for the final version.

Geries Sa'ed Khoury

INTRODUCTION

Before discussing the church in the Holy Land, it is important to make clear who the Christians in the Holy Land are. Today, we have about 120 thousand Arab, indigenous Christians whose Christianity goes back to the very beginning of the Christian faith. This number is divided into about 20 different denominations. Some of them have very few numbers whilst others, such as the Greek-Orthodox, the Greek-Catholics and the Roman Catholics, form the main body of the church. It is worthwhile noting that despite the numerous denominations, the faithful are living in strong social unity as a result of sharing a common language, tradition, history and social problems.

These Christians are living in a very complicated cultural context and, as a small minority, they face many problems. Since these numerous difficulties remain unsolved many of these Christians emigrate to Europe and the U.S.A. An illustration of this emigration is that in 1948 Jerusalem was populated by 26.000 Christians whilst today it has only 9.000. In a few years' time, if this situation continues, the churches will become nothing more than museums visited by Western pilgrims. This was a fear expressed by Pope Paul VI when he visited the Holy Land in 1964.

The principle concern for the local church and its leaders in the Holy Land is to work seriously to keep the local church alive, so that it is a church of people and not a church of stones. Such work can already be observed in local education, in schools and universities, in numerous health institutions and social centers and in homes and housing projects.

THE CHURCH OF JERUSALEM

The Church of Jerusalem in the Holy Land is the mother of all churches. This is because it is the first church, established at Pentecost when the Holy Spirit descended upon the Apostles. The Apostles in Jerusalem prayed together, shared everything in common and started to teach the words of our Lord. They spoke to the people with all the freshness of that life.

When the disciples increased, the Church of Jerusalem, the mother of all churches, was organized with Apostles who led it, elders who administered it, and deacons who served it.

Today, the church of the Holy Land is an Oriental church which differs from the Occidental churches, Catholic and Protestant, by its history, traditions and rites and by its spiritual richness.

This church exists today in the Holy Land with her sisters of the West both Roman Catholic and

Protestant, in love and cooperation, serving the one Body of Christ.

In these few pages, we cannot discuss the history of the church in detail. It is a beautiful history on the one hand, because it speaks of the spreading of God's Word in this part of the world and sad on the other hand because the church was divided for theological and political reasons. So the one history became several histories.

HISTORY OF THE DIVISION
OF THE CHURCH

The church began to divide at the beginning of the fourth century with the spread of heresies and the erroneous teaching of the faith. The first problem that faced the church was Arius' teaching which can be summarized as follows:-

1. There is one God. He alone is Unbegotten and Eternal.
2. This absolute and transcendent God cannot communicate His being completely and so in no true sense can God have a son coequal with Himself.
3. Jesus is not God, he was adopted by God as His son.

These teachings were condemned at the Council of Nicea in the year 325. At this council the Church formulated and affirmed the Nicene Creed. Arius and his friends were exiled outside the borders of the Roman Empire.

After the council, the Church met in Constantinople in the year 381 to reconcile the Semi-Arians with the church and to put an end to the Macedonian Heresy. The council declared the perfect humanity of Christ and confirmed the Nicene Creed. But in the year 431 the church was convoked to a council at Ephesus to condemn the heresy of Nestorius who taught that Jesus of Nazareth and the divine Word were two distinct persons. The unity between the two natures he maintained is an external and moral union, so the incarnation is nothing more than the indwelling of the Word in a man. Accordingly, Mary is not the Mother of God (Theotokos), but of a man, Christ (Christokos).

The council affirmed again the Nicene Creed and concerning the nature of Christ the council taught that in him two perfect and distinct natures were united in one person. The council also affirmed that Mary is the Mother of God(Theotokos). As a result of this council the church was divided between Nestorianism and non-Nestorianism. This latter became the Orthodox faith.

Today there is a Nestorian Church in Syria, Iraq, India and one of its branches is the Chaldean Church which has a representative in the Holy Land. The Council of Ephesus initiated a new but sad chapter in the history of the church, one marked by divisions.

But the greatest tragedy in the history of the church was the result of the Council of Chalcedon (451). In the middle of the fifth century, the church met once more to look into Eutichus' teachings. According to this, the human nature in Christ instead of retaining its own proper activity and identity was completely absorbed by the divine.

This doctrine was known as monophysitism or the "one nature". The teaching of Eutichus was condemned by the fathers of the council, held at Chalcedon in 451 and they confirmed that in Christ two perfect and distinct natures were united in one person.

In honesty it must be said that the division of the church into two parts, Chalcedonian and non-Chalcedonian, was caused not only by theological, but also by political differences. The non-Chalcedonians today do not wish to be called monophysites but non-Chalcedonians. It was admitted recently by the Chalcedonians that the differences which divide the two churches are verbal rather than a matter of faith. This can be seen from the joint declaration made in Rome in 1973 by Pope Paul VI and the Coptic Patriarch Amba Shenouda III:- "In accordance with our apostolic traditions transmitted to our Churches and preserved therein, and in conformity with the early three ecumenical councils, we confess one faith in the one Triune God, the divinity of the Only Begotten Son of God, the Second Person of the Holy Trinity, The Word of God, the effulgence of His glory and the express image of His substance, who for us was incarnate, assuming for Himself a real body with a rational soul, and who shared with us our humanity but without sin. We confess that our Lord and God and Saviour and King of us all, Jesus Christ, is perfect God with respect to His Divinity, perfect man with respect to His humanity. In Him His divinity is united with His humanity in a real, perfect union without mingling, without commixtion, without confusion, without alteration, without division, without separation. His divinity did not separate from His humanity for an instant, not for the twinkling of an eye. He who is God eternal and invisible became visible in the flesh, and took upon Himself the form of a servant. In Him are preserved all the properties of the divinity and all the properties of the humanity, together in a real, perfect, indivisible and inseparable union."

The non-Chalcedonian churches existing in the Orient are Coptic, Ethiopian, Syrian and Armenian Churches, all of which exist in the Holy Land as we shall see later on.

The non-Chalcedonians called the church that accepted the Chalcedonian definition "Melkites" because their faith was endorsed by Marcian , the Roman Emperor (Malka).

In the year 1054 because of a political power struggle between East and West, the Patriarch of Constantinople was excommunicated by the Pope. Subsequently the other three Oriental Patriarchates (Alexandria, Antioch and Jerusalem) followed Constantinople. This painful division between East and West persists until today.

The Oriental Orthodox Church itself did not remain united because some longed for union with the Roman Catholic Church. This was the result of the work of Catholic missionaries who came to the East and also because of internal problems.

One particular division in the Oriental Orthodox Church occurred in the year 1724 when a group within the Orthodox Church of Antioch expressed, in complete independence, its wish to be in communion with the Church of Rome. This group became known as Greek Melkite Catholics. The non-Chalcedonian church was also divided because some wished to unite with the Church of Rome.

Here we should mention that unfortunately the Western church did not remain united. Since the voices that cried for reform and the restoration of the purity and testimony of the church were not heeded, the result was the division between the Roman Catholic and the churches of the Reformation.

What concerns us mainly is the Oriental church which exists in the Holy Land, but we cannot discuss this church without mentioning its relationship with the other churches such as the Roman Catholic, the Anglicans and the Protestants.

The churches in the Holy Land can be summarized as follows:-

1. The Nestorian Church which refuses the decisions of the third ecumenical council at Ephesus.

2. The churches which only acknowledge the first three ecumenical councils but reject the Chalcedonian and following councils. These are the Coptic, Syrian, Armenian and Ethiopian Churches.

3. The Orthodox Church which acknowledges only the first seven ecumenical councils.

4. The Oriental Catholic Churches which consist of groups originally belonging to the Oriental Orthodox Churches, but which felt that they needed to have union with the Roman Catholic Church. These churches are Greek Catholic, Maronite, Syrian Catholic, Coptic Catholic, and Armenian Catholic. They still keep their rites, traditions, customs, theology and spirituality and they are still Oriental in their culture and administration.

5. The Roman Catholic Church which is today the church accepting all the ecumenical councils.
6. The Anglican and Protestant Churches which separated from the Roman Catholic Church at the Reformation.

When we speak, therefore, of the Oriental church in general and of the various denominations in the Holy Land in particular, it is insufficient to distinguish their heritage and their differences from the Western church by using «Catholic» or «Orthodox».

Without a doubt the Roman Catholic Church which exists in the Middle East differs in its traditions from the Oriental Catholic Church, and the Protestant Church differs from both of these.

Today, all the churches in the Holy Land, like the pieces of an incomplete mosaic picture, are longing and praying for the restoration of the whole picture, the unity of Christ's body.

THE ORIENTAL RITES

The word «rite» means the form of prayers, symbols and actions which is used by the faithful in order to express their adoration. The rite is the outward expression, given by the church, of the inner worship of God. The rite, therefore, gives shape and guidance to the life of the church.

The object of the rite is to celebrate the divine liturgy, offer the formal prayers, and to administer the Sacraments. In other words, the rite in each church is the group expression of faith. The various Oriental rites which are rich in spirituality are part of the national and cultural tradition of the people as we shall see.

At the beginning of the Christian era, the church had several rites since the Apostles did not impose a particular rite for all Christians. So the local leaders had complete freedom in establishing the church's way of prayer. There was some similarity between these rites in the second and third centuries when Greek was the language used.

Later on it is possible to differentiate between the rites according to the geographical locations of the church. It is not possible here to talk about all the different rites in detail. However, the five main Oriental rites must be mentioned briefly.

They are:-

1. **The Byzantine rite:** An ancient rite which is used by the Eastern Orthodox Churches and by some of the Oriental Catholic Churches, for example the Greek Catholics.

    Its language was originally only Greek. Today there are different languages in which the Byzantine liturgy is celebrated such as Arabic, Russian, Romanian and other western languages. It has three different liturgies: the main one is the divine and holy liturgy of the father among the saints, John Chrysostom, while the divine liturgy of St. Basil the Great is celebrated ten times a year and the divine liturgy of Gregory the theologian, also called the liturgy of the Presanctified, is celebrated during the great Lent. In addition to these three liturgies the Byzantine tradition contains different services and numerous prayers, composed mostly by the fathers of the church.

2. **The Armenian rite:**-The rite of the Armenian Orthodox and Catholic Church which is followed today by all the Armenian Churches wherever they may be. It is the only rite that has no subdivisions. Its richness arises from the different influences on its prayers and ceremonies from other Oriental rites and by its importance as a national rite for the Armenian Orthodox and Catholics. The beauty of this rite can be seen in its mystical prayers and its fascinating hymns. The language is Armenian, but today as a result of the Armenian diaspora, the liturgy is celebrated in different languages in order to give to the Armenians who are not acquainted with their mother language the opportunity of participating in the Holy Service.

3. **The Alexandrian rite:** This rite replaced a variety of local Egyptian rites. Today it is the rite of the Orthodox, Catholic Coptic and Ethiopian Churches. This rite is characterized by long prayers which are rich in their diversity.

This variety includes reading the prayers written by the fathers of the church such as Saint Antony the founder of Monasticism. They also read from both Old and New Testaments. During each liturgy, there are readings from the Psalms,the Bible and particularly from Paul's letters. The spirituality of this rite like the other rites is rich in prayers to the Virgin and the Saints.

4. **The Chaldean rite:** One of its forms is the Chaldean or Assyrian rite which was originally used by the Persian Church and spread to India with Nestorian beliefs.

5. **The Antiochian rite:** This rite is one of the oldest in the East and was used by the whole church of Antioch. Its language is Syriac and, like all Oriental rites, it is characterized by numerous prayers taken from the Syrian fathers of the church such as St. Efram who is considered a pillar in this tradition. The liturgical richness of the Syrian rite can be appreciated in the many invocations to our

Lord, to the Holy Mother of God, to the Holy Trinity and to the Martyr Saints. Three different rites in use today emerged from it:

a. The Syrian rite which is used by both Catholic and Orthodox Syrians. It is the closest to the original Antiochian rite.

b. The Maronite rite which is a form of the Antiochian rite. It has undergone a slight adaptation having to do with the development of the Maronite Church and today some changes have also been made because of its close relationship with the Latin or Roman Catholic Church.

Its Language is Syriac, but today the church uses Arabic or other languages understood by the faithful where there is no acquaintance with Syriac.

c. The Malankar rite which is used in India by some of the descendants of the Nestorian Church.

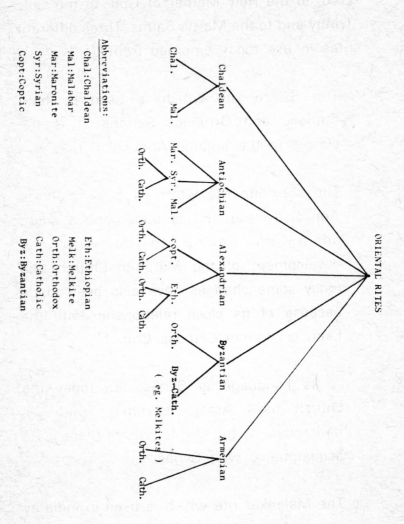

ORIENTAL RITES

Chaldean
- Chal.
- Mal.

Antiochian
- Orth.
- Cath. Syr.
- Mal.

Alexandrian
- Orth.
- Cath. Copt.
- Orth.
- Cath. Eth.

Byzantian
- Orth.
- Byz-Cath. (eg. Melkites)

Armenian
- Orth.
- Cath.

Abbreviations:

Chal:Chaldean
Mal:Malabar
Mar:Maronite
Syr:Syrian
Copt:Coptic

Eth:Ethiopian
Melk:Melkite
Orth:Orthodox
Cath:Catholic
Byz:Byzantian

ORIENTAL SPIRITUALITY

Despite the variety of rites in the Oriental churches there is a unity in their spirituality. The Westerner who attends the rites of these Oriental churches is amazed at the beauty of the sung prayers and by the complexity that he sees in the liturgy. But he is most moved by the deep sharing of the faithful in their prayers. One of the most beautiful descriptions of the Oriental divine liturgy, comes from the Russian theologian Nicolas Zernov:

" The Oriental liturgy is the fountain of inspiration of the Oriental Christians. The liturgy appeals to all the human senses; the eyes of the faithful admire the beauty of the holy icons. His ears listen to hymns. The incense surrounds him with aromatic perfume, his body glorifies the Creator with symbolic acts and his spirit is elevated for the adoration of the heavenly Father ".

Zernov's description is not an exaggeration. During the Oriental liturgy the people live the fullness of their faith as they pray and learn simultaneously.

Oriental piety is ascetic and mystical, it is contemplative and passionate, it is liturgical and communicative. The main theme of the liturgical prayers is the recognition of personal sin. This recognition expresses the confident relationship between man and God. During the Oriental liturgy

Christ the Pantocrator

and the numerous other prayers, we can appreciate the manifestation of the people's love towards Jesus Christ and see the filial relationship between the faithful and God with the Holy Mother and all the Saints as they invoke their help.

Within the Byzantine rite which is rich in prayers and liturgies, the church sings the fundamental mysteries of the Trinity and of the Incarnation. We can also say that the prayer in this liturgy concerns the whole life of Jesus Christ from His birth to His triumphant resurrection from death.

In other words, the Byzantine liturgy is the medium through which the worshipper reaches God.

When we speak about Oriental spirituality we can say that beyond the feeling of the grandeur of the prayers and the liturgical words, the aim of it all is the divinization of the person as announced in the Gospel. This is the main element in Oriental spirituality.

Such a divinization can be obtained only through the union of the person with the life of the Trinity through Jesus Christ.

In Oriental spirituality both private and public prayers offer to each one the seeds of contemplation he needs and in return the church expects of each one a close participation in its prayers of praise and thanksgiving.

Consequently, Oriental spirituality is not simply the traditional practice of a rite but involves the participation of the faithful, and becomes the basis of their understanding of community and sharing.

It is mystical, because of the eager activity of the soul attempting to reach out after spiritual realities and it is universal because her bridegroom is Jesus Christ, the prototype of the whole cosmos.

Mary the Mother of God has a special place in Oriental spirituality because, through Her, God communicated Himself to His creatures through the Holy Mystery of Incarnation.

You will be surprised when visiting the Oriental churches. Their architectural structure, their beautiful icons and their fascinating frescoes are

Our lady of Vladimir

channels of divine grace, as John of Damascus said.

The icon is a symbol of Oriental theology and facilitates the contact between the divine and the human.

In the Oriental churches the iconastasis(the screen between the altar and the people) holds the

Greek Catholic Church of the Annunciation showing the Iconastas

icons which illustrate the mystery of Christ which is celebrated in the liturgy.

The spiritual life of the Oriental churches differs from that of the Occidental churches by its stress on contemplation and its lifting up of the spirit in its yearning to reach God.

THE GREEK ORTHODOX PATRIARCHATE OF JERUSALEM

When we speak about the Greek Orthodox Church, we mean the church which believes that it is the true church of Christ because of its continuity with divine revelation and because of its original apostolic tradition. In this country the Orthodox Church of Jerusalem is considered the mother of all churches.

When we refer to this church, we recognize it as the sole church to admit, recognize and believe in the doctrines of the first seven ecumenical councils. The first council was Nicea in the year 325 and the seventh was Nicea II, in 787.

After the seventh council, and for political and cultural reasons, relations between the Patriarchate of Rome and the Patriarchate of Constantinople deteriorated. This resulted in a permanent schism, in 1054. It also subsequently separated Alexandria, Antioch and Jerusalem from Rome.

After this date an unsuccessful series of tentative approaches were made towards reconciling the Orthodox East and the Catholic West. They included the council of Lyon in 1274 and the council of Florence in 1439 at which the misunderstanding between them was not ecclesiastical but rather political and cultural.

In 1453, when Constantinople fell into the hands of the Turks, the Patriarch of Constantinople and all other Oriental Patriarchs were under the Turkish rule. The possibility of reconciliation and unity with Rome was therefore lessened; a situation which continues up to this day, despite the existing dialogue between the Orthodox and the Catholic Church which started after the historic meeting between the Pope of Rome Paul VI and the Ecumennical Partriarch of Constantinople Athenagoras.

In the Holy Land, the Greek Orthodox community is one of the largest Christian groups. The Patriarch is assisted by a holy Synod. The Patriarch, bishops and monks form the Brotherhood of the Holy Sepulchre and all of them are Greeks.

The parishes are served by married Arab priests. The faithful are approximately 40.000 living in Galilee and the West Bank.

The Patriarchate of Jerusalem was established by the council of Chalcedon in 451 and is one of four ancient Oriental Patriarchates: Constantinople, Antioch, Alexandria and Jerusalem. It is one of the fourteen autocephalous Orthodox Churches in the world. However, the Ecumenical Patriarch of Constantinople is the honorary head of these Orthodox Churches.

Today the Patriarchate has the most rights over the Holy Places according to the Status Quo which was issued by the Turkish Sultan in 1852. As a result, the Brotherhood of the Holy Sepulchre is responsible for the protection of the Holy Shrines and the Orthodox monasteries in the Holy Land.

THE RUSSIAN CHURCH

In 988, the Grand Duke Vladimir of Kiev was converted to Christianity and adopted the Greek Orthodox faith as the Religion of the State.

Later on, in the eleventh century, there is evidence that some Russian Christian pilgrims went to the Holy Land. For centuries after this, the Russians visited the Holy Land without having official ecclesiastical or political representatives.

In 1820, a Russian consulate was opened in Jaffa. Its aim was to protect and maintain contact with Russian pilgrims. In 1841, the first Russian emissary Archimandrite Cyril, arrived in the Holy Land in order to study the situation of the local church and to make recommendations as to how the Arab Orthodox faithful could be helped. He did not achieve great success, and for political and financial difficulties he returned to Russia. In 1843, the Russian Church sent another emissary Archimandrite Porphyri with a small budget to help the Arab Orthodox people. He also achieved very little. He was able, however, to gain a great sympathy from the Arab Orthodox community and started good relations with the Orthodox Patriarchate. He went back to Russia to collect money from interested individuals. With this money he came back to Jerusalem and started to purchase land in order to build churches, schools and hostels.

In 1848 he established a seminary for Arab religious teachers.

In 1857, the Russian church decided to send a Bishop as head of the Russian missionaries in the Holy Land. In 1858, Cyril, the only Russian bishop arrived in Jerusalem and the Russian Ecclesiastical mission was founded. Then in 1881, the missionary Orthodox Palestenian Society was founded. It aimed at assisting the Russian Church and at purchasing land and monuments.

With the intensification of the work of the Russian Church in the Holy Land, it became one of the most active within the local community. It gained a lot of property, land, buildings, monasteries, churches, medical centers, hostels, schools and seminaries. All this was for the benefit of the local community.

The Russian Church, with the establishment of the state of Israel and the Six Day War, lost a lot of its buildings and property.

This church has never had a community of Arab Christians in the Holy Land because its main aim has always been mission.

Amongst the beautiful Russian Churches in Jerusalem, there are the churches of St. Mary Magdalene in Gethsemane and of the Ascension on the Mount of Olives.

There are two Russian groups in the Holy Land today: one in communion with the Patriarchate in Moscow; the other related to the Russian Orthodox Church in exile. Both communities are led by an Archimandrite, assisted by a number of monks and nuns.

THE RUMANIAN CHURCH

The Rumanian Church is an autocephalous orthodox church. It claims an apostolic origin. This is because the Rumanians do not exclude the possibility that Paul had contacts with the people of Thrace and other areas, from which the Rumanian population claims its origin. They base this suggestion on Romans 15:19 where we find a description of Paul's ministry: "from Jerusalem all the way around to Illyricum"

The Rumanian Church in the Holy Land was founded in 1935. In Jerusalem, the church is located between the West and the East side of the city. It is a small church but beautifully decorated. The church in Jerusalem is headed by a Rumanian Archimandrite monk who is assisted by a small community of monks and nuns.

The Rumanian Church follows the Byzantine tradition in its liturgical life and its spirituality, using the Rumanian language.

THE SYRIAN ORTHODOX CHURCH

The Syrians are the grandsons of the ancient Arameans who inhabited Greater Syria. They were the first to embrace Christianity, and the name «Aramean» was replaced by «Syrian» after their conversion to Christianity in order to forget their Pagan name.

This church is one of the non-Chalcedonian churches. After 451 it grew rapidly in Syria and Iraq. It made a notable contribution to theological literature especially after the coming of Islam. From Syria it spread to the Far East and especially to India where it formed a very large community. Today this community is divided into two parts: one belonging to the Syrian Patriarch residing in Damascus and the other under a local Mafrian. (In the Syrian Orthodox heirarchy a Mafrian is immediately below the Patriarch). There is also a small number of Syrian Orthodox dioceses in the west, especially in the Americas.

This church is considered amongst the oldest churches in the Holy Land. The church still uses the Syriac language in its liturgy and prayers. They use the liturgy of St. James, the first bishop of Jerusalem, in addition to a variety of other liturgies.

The church also has numerous books for prayers, most of which are related to or belong to the fathers of the church such as St. Efram. All these are according to the Syrian rite.

In the Holy Land the church is headed by a bishop who resides in the Monastery of St. Mark where there is also the church of St. Mark. According to Syrian tradition, the monastery and the church were built on the ruins of the site of the Last Supper. The site also has links with important events such as the Feet Washing and Pentecost.

The Patriarch of Antioch and all the East is the supreme head of the Universal Syrian Orthodox Church. He is elected by the Synod of bishops and resides today in Damascus. He is the head of the Universal Syrian Church to which the bishopric of the Syrian Church in the Holy Land belongs.

In the Holy Land the Syrian Orthodox Church has privileges in the Holy Places. For example, in the Church of the Nativity it has an altar and in the Holy Sepulchre Church it has a chapel. Today the Syrian Orthodox Church numbers about 1,000 and most of them live in Jerusalem and Bethlehem.

THE COPTIC ORTHODOX CHURCH

The church of Egypt was founded by St. Mark who was the head of the church in Alexandria which later became one of the oldest Oriental Patriarchates. In this country and especially in Alexandria,fathers of the church such as Clement, Origen and Athanasius were teachers of great prestige at the famous Alexandrian Theological School.

The Egyptian Church, which is known today by the name Coptic (this name came from the Greek name of the inhabitants of Egypt Αἰγύπτος) did not accept the teaching of Chalcedon. This controversy was due to theological formulae and political pressure. Its opposition to the council of Chalcedon and to the king who supported it, helped the church to maintain its unity under the administration of its Patriarch. He resided at that time in Alexandria, but today he is based in Cairo.

The Coptic Church is known as a monophysite church (believing in one nature in Jesus Christ), a description which is not really correct. In its theology and in its beliefs, we can see clearly that this church does believe in two separate and distinct natures in Jesus Christ: the divine and the human.

Today the biggest Coptic community is in Egypt where it consists of about six million people. The head of the church is the Patriarch who is called "Pope" and who is helped by a council of bishops.

The Coptic Church established its ties with the Holy Land a long time ago. This relation began in a special way in the fourth century after the foundation of the monastic life by St. Antony. It grew with the building of Coptic churches in the Holy Land after the nineth century. The Islamic Arab period, however, diminished the growth of the Coptic Church both in Egypt and the Holy Land.

The Copts were treated equally with the other Oriental Churches in Jerusalem during the Crusader period. This situation changed with the coming of Salah-ed-Din to Jerusalem in 1187.

The Copts maintained their activities and worked to fortify their church and their community.

The support of the Mamlouks, a powerful group of Muslims from Egypt, helped the church to achieve this. In this period, the Alexandrian Patriarch Cyril III (1235-1242) sent a bishop as his representative to Jerusalem, and since that time, the Alexandrian Patriarch has been represented officially by a bishop in the Holy Land.

Today, in addition to the churches and monasteries, the Copts enjoy such rights as having their own chapels in the Holy Places, especially in the churches of the Nativity and the Holy Sepulchre.

The community is small with about 800 faithful living in Jerusalem, Bethlehem and Nazareth under the supervision of a Bishop who resides in Jerusalem at the Coptic Monastery. He is assisted by monks, who take care of the holy places and the pastoral life of the faithful.

The Coptic Church follows its own rite, the Alexandrian rite, which is rich in prayers and spirituality. The language of this rite is Coptic but sometimes Arabic and other languages are used to facilitate communication with the faithful.

THE ETHIOPIAN CHURCH

Historians of the church mention the coming of Ethiopian pilgrimages to the Holy Land as early as the fourth century. There is also evidence for the presence of a strong Ethiopian community in Jerusalem in the Middle Ages and during the fourteenth and fifteenth centuries. We have plenty of evidence about their presence here, such as letters from the Ethiopian Emperors to their monks in Jerusalem.

The Ethiopians have two chapels inside the Church of the Holy Sepulchre, privileges in Bethlehem and in the Tomb of the Holy Virgin at Gethsemane, a monastery at the Cave of David on Mount Zion and other properties.

The Church has its own rite in its own language. This is related to the Alexandrian rite, according to which, the liturgy (Qeddase) is celebrated. The unique characteristic of the Ethiopian rite is that it has a monthly repetition of major feasts such as the Feast of the Holy Trinity, St. Michael the Archangel, Our Lady, Nativity, Passion of Christ....etc.

Another characteristic of the Ethiopian spirituality is the way in which the faithful seek God. It is mostly an individual and private way. They repeat certain prayers, referring to God and the Saints, and read the scripture especially the Gospel of St. John and the psalms. The monks use a book which is called the (Book of Monks) which is composed of three different books.

This is in addition to the common prayer in which all the members of the community take part.

Today, the Ethiopians in the Holy Land are a small community which consists mostly of monks and nuns. Some laity are also with the community.

THE ARMENIAN ORTHODOX CHURCH

St. Gregory the illuminator was an Armenian and had converted the king of Armenia, Tiridatis III, in about the year 301. Thus Armenia was the first nation to accept Christianity as the state religion. This encouraged relations between Armenia and Palestine and pilgrimage to Jerusalem, the city of salvation, grew rapidly. Closer relations between the two countries had therefore been started. Since the fifth century, an Armenian religious community was present in Jerusalem and they played a vital role in the monastic life in Palestine. They also played an important role in keeping the Holy Places during the Persian invasion of Jerusalem and then under Arab rule (638-1099). Their position until the arrival of the Crusaders was better than that of the other Oriental Churches owing to an agreement between the Armenian Kingdom of Cilicia and the Frankish Kingdom. In the Turkish period, the Armenians were the custodians of the Holy Places along with the Latins and the Greek Orthodox. But between the seventeenth and the nineteenth centuries the Armenians were in their hardest and darkest period, especially with regard to their jurisdiction in the Holy Places. This situation was changed with the declaration of the Status Quo in 1852 which reconfirmed the rights and the privileges of the Armenians in the Holy Places as they have them in our present time.

The Armenian Church recognised the first three Ecumenical Councils. For political reasons, however, it was prevented by the Persians and Byzantines from participating in the council of Chalcedon in 451. Later on the Armenian Church declared its support of the non-Chalcedonian churches and in 526, it claimed its official separation from the Byzantine Church. Since this date the Armenian Church has been independent with its own history, theology, rite and spiritual heritage.

During the Western missionary movement amongst the Oriental Churches, some of the Armenians showed them their sympathy and Efram the Patriarch of Constantinople persecuted all those who had good relations with the Catholics. This situation went on until 1742 when Abraham Arzafian was consecrated as a Patriarch to the Armenian Catholics in the East.

Today the Armenian Orthodox church has a Katholicos in Etchmiadzin (Soviet Armenia), a Katholicos in Antelias (Lebanon), and Patriarchs in Jerusalem and Istanbul. The Katholicos in Etchmiadzin has supreme authority in the Armenian church.

Today the Armenian Orthodox Patriarchate in the Holy Land possesses the famous Armenian compound in Jerusalem occupying the entire summit of Mount Zion which is almost one fifth of the area of the old city. In this area is the Cathedral of St. James, the residence of the Patriarch, the living quarters of the community, the theological seminary, the Convent and Church of the Holy Archangels.

At the beginning of this century the Armenians were massacred and driven out of Armenia by the Turks. A large number emigrated to the Holy Land and the community here grew to a large number.

For different political and economic reasons they have since many left the country.

The Armenian Orthodox community in the Holy Land today therefore numbers around 2000.

THE LATIN PATRIARCHATE

After Christianity had been carried to the West by the Apostles and especially to Rome by Peter and Paul, the Roman Empire treated the adherents of this faith with hostility for three centuries. Despite this attitude, the Empire eventually became christianized under Constantine.

However, there is clear evidence in the Holy Land that some Romans believed in Christianity from the very beginning. These belonged to the local church under the Jurisdiction of the four patriarchates of Alexandria, Antioch, Constantinople and Jerusalem. The Latins, therefore, did not have their own independent administration. This was inspite of the dominance of Rome until the seventh century.

In the year 638, the Caliph Omar Ibn al-Khattab entered Jerusalem, and the Patriarch Sophronius gave him the keys of the city as a sign of cooperation and peaceful living. From that time until the year 1099 when the Latins took Jerusalem during the first Crusade, the church was under Islamic rule.

In 1099, however, the Latin Patriarchate was officially established in Jerusalem. But, in the year 1187 Jerusalem was reconquered by Salah-el-Din and the Latins fled to Acre.

In 1291, Acre, the last residence of the Crusaders also fell to the Arabs and, the Latin Church was no longer represented officially in the Holy Land.

A short time after the fall of Acre, the Franciscans and several missionary groups arrived in the Holy Land. They did not re-establish the patriarchate but they assured the continuation of the Latin presence.

The two most important reasons for the Latin presence in the Holy Land are:

1. The coming of the Crusaders which helped to convert people from their own tradition to the

Latin tradition.

2. The work of Latin missionaries between the different Oriental communities, resulting in some people adopting the Latin tradition.

In 1874, Pope Pius IX restored the Latin Patriarchate of Jerusalem as a residential See. This was because he wanted to maintain the Latin community in the Holy Land. Moreover, he was alarmed at the increase of Protestant missionaries in the area, especially the coming of the first Anglican bishop to Jerusalem in 1842.

Today, the Patriarchate is headed by a Patriarch who resides in the Old City and who is helped by three Vicars, one in Nazareth, one in Amman and one in Cyprus. They are assisted by a number of priests who are responsible for different pastoral work among the 25.000 members of the Latin community. In addition to these the Franciscans are responsible for many Latin parishes and a number of important activities which benefit the local community.

Since the fourteenth century when the Franciscans came to the Holy Land they have been the custodians of the holy places.

The rite and the spiritual tradition of the Latin Patriarchate is Roman Catholic. It is important, however, to say that all the indigenous faithful are eager to live in their Oriental cultural context.

THE MARONITE CHURCH

The Maronite Church is the only Oriental Church which is entirely Catholic. It is rooted in the Antiochian and Syriac traditions. Our knowledge of its history is not complete.

Its beginnings go back to St. Maroun, who died in 410 and who gave rise to the name Maronite. Before his death, he established a small community on the banks of the Orontus, in Syria where he lived. After his death, the members continued to live there together. In 452 they built a Monastery and a church called (The Monastery of St. Maroun).

Some of the local people participated in their prayers and thereafter were called "Maronites". After the Arab Conquest of Antioch in 636 the Antiochian Patriarch resided in Constantinople. Between 702 and 742, however, this patriarchal seat was vacant. It was this time that the Maronites themselves elected a Patriarch. This Patriarch worked very hard to keep unity between the members of his community. Such was the establishment of the Maronite Patriarchate which was recognized as independent by the time of Caliph Marwan II (744-748).

The two characteristics of this church are its fanatical defence of the teaching of Chalcedon and its good relationship with the Church of Rome after the schism between East and West. This relationship improved during the Crusades and led to official communion with Rome in 1181.

On the other hand, the Maronites tried to keep their Oriental identity by following their own spiritual traditions, by having their own Patriarch who resides today in Bkerke in Lebanon, where the largest Maronite community exists in the Middle East, and by having their own clergy. All this was inspite of continual attempts by Rome to Latinize their Oriental customs.

In the Holy Land today the Maronite community consists of about 6.000 people, most of whom live in Galilee. A Maronite Patriarchal Vicariate was established in Jerusalem in 1895 which at present takes care of the small community living in Jerusalem and its surroundings.

THE GREEK CATHOLIC CHURCH

The characteristics of this church are:
1. Its Oriental spiritual heritage.
2. Its adherence to the Council of Chalcedon.
3. Its communion with the Church of Rome.

Its present position cannot be separated from its spiritual and historical background. The church has a desire to retain its Oriental character and to be in full communion with the Church of Rome.

The Greek Catholic Church is also called the Melkite Church. This name came originally from the Syriac word Malka and it was attributed to it by the non-Chalcedonians because the Orthodoxy of the Chalcedonian Council was endorsed by the Emperor (Malka) Marcian. Only later was it applied to the Greek Catholic Churches.

In 1054, religious, cultural and political factors caused the separation between East and West. Until then, the Byzantine Christians of the

Patriarchate of Antioch were in communion with Rome. After 1054, and for different reasons, especially political, the Byzantine Churches had been reduced to a minority. This deterioration in the position of the Byzantine Churches inspired the Roman Catholic Church to expand its missionary activities in the Middle East. A missionary campaign was launched in the seventeenth century, and well trained and educated Jesuits, Franciscans and others started to work among the members of the Oriental Church, and as a result of spiritual hunger and for economic reasons, many of the Byzantines became sympathizers to the missionaries' work. These were encouraged by the good will of the leaders of the church in Antioch who were by now well disposed towards possible future unity with Rome.

But at the beginning of the eighteenth century, the peaceful coexistence between the pro Roman elements and the Orthodox came to an end and Bishop Euthymios Saifi announced that he wanted to be in communion with Rome. This was the beginning of a canonical schism which occurred within the Patriarchate of Antioch in 1724. This separation was inevitable especially after the double election of a Greek Catholic Patriarch, Cyril Tanas VI (1724-1759) and of the Orthodox Patriarch Sylvester.

For a century the situation of the Melkite Church was uneasy because the Orthodox maltreated them and the Turks did not recognize them as an independent church.

In the nineteenth century the Melkite Patriarch Maximos III Mazloum was able to take up residence in Damascus and in 1846 to obtain official recognition from the Subline Porte as Patriarch and head of the Melkite Church. He established the Patriarchal Vicariate in Jerusalem which he visited and in which he held a synod for the Melkite Church in 1848.

The Greek Catholic diocese in Galilee was established soon after the separation from the Orthodox Church, in the year 1752 with the ordination of Makarios Oujaemi by the Patriarch Cyril VI as the non-resident auxiliary bishop of Acre.

In 1772, the Greek Catholics of Jerusalem and all the Holy Land were put under the Jurisdiction of the Patriarch of Antioch.

Today, the Archbishop's residence is in Haifa and his title is "The Bishop of Acre, Haifa, Nazareth, and all Galilee".

The number of Melkites in the diocese of Galilee is approximately 38.000 and they are grouped in twenty seven parishes. The Greek Catholic diocese of Jerusalem has about 3.300 divided into about eight parishes and headed by a Patriarchal Vicar.

THE SYRIAN CATHOLIC CHURCH

At the beginning of the seventeenth century there were various Catholic missionary activities among the Oriental Churches. As with many of the other churches, some of the Syrian Orthodox showed sympathy to the Catholic Church and its missionaries.

This increased and in the year 1662, Andraus was elected Patriarch by the Syrian Catholic people in Alepo and was recognized by the Sultan Muhamed IV.

On the 22nd of July 1663, he was confirmed by Pope Alexander VII. This was the culmination of a series of events in which the Syrian Orthodox church was separated into two parts: Syrian Orthodox and Syrian Catholic.

Since 1890 the Syrian Catholic Patriarchate in the Holy Land has been represented by a Patriarchal Vicar. He resides in Jerusalem and is responsible for the small Syrian Catholic community which numbers about 350 faithful living in Jerusalem and Bethlehem.

In spite of its union with Rome, the Syrian Catholics retain their Syrian rite and traditions using the Syriac Language.

THE ARMENIAN CATHOLIC CHURCH

This church was separated from the Armenian Orthodox Church in 1742 with the election of Abraham Arzafian as Patriarch of the Armenian Catholics. He resided in Lebanon because the Ottoman Turks forbade him to go to Constantinople, Damascus or Istanbul.

In 1842 he sent a Vicar to Jerusalem as a representative to take care of the Armenian Catholic community which grew rapidly after the Armenian massacre by the Turks. During that time, the Armenian Catholics did not have a residence in the Holy Land. The vicar therefore resided initially in the Latin Patriarchate. Later the Armenian Catholics bought a piece of land and built a residence and a church which was inaugurated in 1905 and which is situated beside the third station on the Via Dolorosa. The Armenian Catholic community in the Holy Land is small and consists of about 600 people.

This church follows the Armenian Orthodox tradition, liturgy and prayers. The only difference is that the Armenian Catholics pray for the Pope.

The church has good relations with the Armenian Orthodox community and they both cooperate for the benefit of the local community.

The desire of this church is to continue to live as an Armenian Church and to be in communion with the Roman Catholic Church.

THE COPTIC CATHOLIC CHURCH

At the beginning of the sixteenth century the Roman Catholics found sympathy with the Orthodox Coptic Church in Egypt.

Their relationship with Rome was unofficial until the year 1899 when a Coptic Catholic Patriarch was elected. His name was Cyril Makar and he was confirmed by Pope Leo the XII and the Patriarchal seat was established in Alexandria.

Today the Coptic Catholic Church has Five dioceses in Egypt: Alexandria, Al—Ismailiyah, Menia, Suhaj and AL—Oqsur. They keep their own Coptic tradition and follow the Alexandrian rite. In 1955 a Coptic Catholic Patriarchal Vicariate was founded in Jerusalem and the Patriarchal Vicar resides in the Old City. He is responsible for a few members in this country, about 35 in all.

THE CHALDEAN CHURCH

The Chaldeans are descendants of the Nestorian (Assyrian) Church which grew rapidly outside the borders of the Roman Empire, and especially in Persia, after the council of Ephesus in 431.

From Persia at the beginning of the seventh century the Nestorians started to spread their teachings outside the country. They spread to Turkistan, China and India which became the center of the Nestorian Church, whilst in Syria and Iraq their work deteriorated.

The Nestorians in India began to make contacts with the Catholic missionary groups who arrived there in the thirteenth century.

In 1552,a group of them refused to accept the election of the Patriarch Simon VIII Denha and claimed their unity with the Roman Church.

In 1553 John Sulaqa was elected as Patriarch

and confirmed by the Pope on twentieth of April in the same year.

Such was the beginning of the Patriarchate of the Catholic Chaldeans.

Today, the See of the Patriarch is in Bagdad. The Chaldean Church is small and exists in India, Syria, Iraq and in other different countries in the West. It consists of only about 250.000 faithful throughout the world. This church follows the Chaldean rite.

In the Holy Land the Chaldean Church is represented by a Patriarchal Vicar. The presence of this representative goes back to the beginning of this century.

However, the Chaldeans do not have a community in the Holy Land today.

THE PROTESTANT CHURCHES

Because the aim of this work is to introduce the local Oriental Churches to Western pilgrims, I thought that there is no need to give extensive information about the different Protestant and Evangelical Churches. But I do wish to write briefly about the presence of these churches in the Holy Land.

At the beginning of the nineteenth century, non-Catholic Western missionaries began to arrive in the Middle East in order to study the situation and to work among the different communities: Christians, Moslems and Jews.

The first notable presence of non-Catholic missionaries in the Holy Land was the result of the Anglo-Prussian coalition which provided the basis of the Anglican bishopric in Jerusalem. This was due to the fact that William IV, the Prussian King agreed with Queen Victoria to establish a joint bishopric in the Holy Land and to be held by an

Anglican and to be alternately nominated by the British and Prussian crown.

In 1841, an Anglican bishop was designated, Michael Solomon Alexander, who made his official entry to Jerusalem on January 21, 1842.

Of course, his presence was not well received at first by the Oriental Churches who were afraid that they might lose their faithful members. This was because of their painful experience with Catholic missionaries in the Middle East in the sixteenth century. Secondly, the designation of the Anglican bishop in the Holy Land was understood by the Roman Catholics as a provocation which aimed to undermine the Latin and Oriental Catholics.

The result was the restoration of the Latin Patriarchate in Jerusalem in the year 1847. Even so, the Anglicans started their work, educational and medical activity especially was developed in many cities in the Holy Land. At the same time Anglican missionaries started to work originally converting Jewish people to Christianity and later on among the different Christian denominations. As a result, a large number became Anglicans and today the Anglican Church is the largest with about 2000 members. This community is served by Arab Anglican priests who take care of different kinds of pastoral work. In 1976, the first Arab bishop was consecrated Bishop in Jerusalem, and resides at the Cathedral of St. George .

In 1887, the Anglo-Prussian coalition came to an end. The Lutherans had built a chapel in 1871, at the Muristan area, in the vicinity of the Church of the Holy Sepulchre, and they used it until the year 1898 when they completed the building of the Church of the Redeemer which is considered today the center of the Lutheran work in the Holy Land.

The head of this community is an Arab bishop who is assisted by local pastors who serve the Lutheran community in different places in the Holy Land and take care of different types of pastoral work. The members of the Lutheran community number around 1000 in the Holy Land today.

Beside the Anglicans and the Lutherans, there are Baptists in the Holy Land. Their origins go back to the year 1911, when a native Palestinian Arab, Shukri Mousa, came back from the United States to his home in Safad in order to initiate Baptist work. Despite many insults and strong opposition from the local Christians towards his work, a small group of Baptists gathered around him in Nazareth where he established the oldest Baptist community in the Middle East. Of course, the reason for the strong opposition to the Baptist work at the beginning was because the local churches were afraid of losing their members.

The Baptists say their aim is to proclaim the Gospel of Jesus Christ in such a way as to call people to repentance and faith in Him as a Saviour and Lord, and to gather such believers for worship, instruction, and training for witness and service in the world.

The members of the Baptist congregation in the Holy Land number about 400. Most of these live in Galilee and a few in Jerusalem.

Other Protestant groups came to the Middle East with different aims. One example is the

Mennonites. The vision which brought the Mennonites to the Middle East was their concern to be a Christian resource for meeting human need. In 1920 they came to Lebanon to assist the Armenian refugees and in 1950 to Jordan to aid the displaced Palestinians and to the Holy Land in 1953 to serve with the church. Their primary work is emergency relief and development projects and this is in addition to educational work in different villages and cities in the Holy Land. Their centre is located in Jerusalem.

It is impossible to cover all the Protestant groups and their activities in the Holy Land. It is important to stress overall, however, that it is the hope of the local Christians that the Protestant groups will serve to strengthen the indigenous church in the Holy Land and work for its unity in Christ.

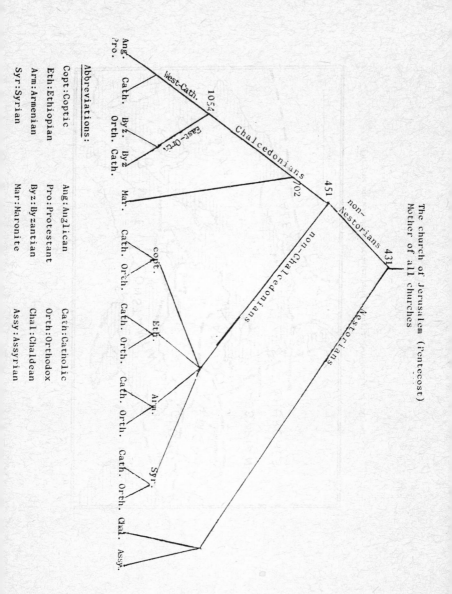

The church of Jerusalem (Pentecost)
Mother of all churches

431

non-Nestorians

Nestorians

451

Chalcedonians

non-Chalcedonians

702

1054

West-Cath.

East-Orth.

Mar.

Copt.

Eth.

Arm.

Syr.

Ang.
Pro.

Cath.

Byz.
Orth.

Byz.
Cath.

Cath. Orth.

Cath. Orth.

Cath. Orth.

Cath. Orth. Chal. Assy.

Abbreviations:

Copt:Coptic
Eth:Ethiopian
Arm:Armenian
Syr:Syrian

Ang:Anglican
Pro:Protestant
Byz:Byzantian
Mar:Maronite

Cath:Catholic
Orth:Orthodox
Chal:Chaldean
Assy:Assyrian

-73-

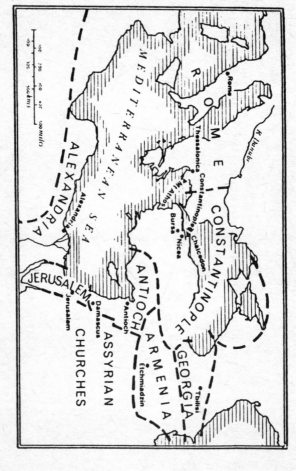

1 *The five ancient Patriarchates, and Georgia, Armenia and Assyria.*

LOCATION OF COMMUNITIES REFERRED TO IN THIS BOOK in JERUSALEM

GREEK ORTHODOX:
Holy Sepulchre
St. Jacob's Cathedral.

RUSSIAN:
St. Mary Magdalene
Gethsmane

RUMANIAN:
Shivtei Israel Str. 46

SYRIAN ORTHODOX:
St. Mark's Convent,
St. Mark's Street

COPTIC ORTHODOX
St. Anthony (Patriarchate),
9th Station

ETHIOPIAN ORTHODOX:

Deir-es-Sultan (H. Sep.)

ARMENIAN ORTHODOX:

St. James Cathedral:

Jaffa Gate

ROMAN CATHOLICS:

Latin Patriarchate

Latin Patriarchate Road.

GREEK CATHOLICS MELKITES

Greek - Catholic Patriarchate

Greek - Catholic Patriarchate Road.

MARONITES:

Maronite Vicariate.

Maronite Str. 25.

SYRIAN CATHOLICS:

Syrian Catholic Church.

Chaldean Str.

ARMENIAN CATHOLICS:

Armenian Catholic Church
Via Dolorosa, III Station.

COPTIC CATHOLICS:

Coptic Catholic Church
St. Francis Str.

CHALDEAN CATHOLICS:

Chaldean Catholic Church
Chaldean Str.

ANGLICANS:

St. George's Cathedral
Nablus Road.

LUTHERANS:

Lutheran Church of the Redeemer
The Old City, Muristan Rd.

BAPTISTS:

4 Narkiss St.,New City.

JERUSALEM — Tomb of Christ

JERUSALEM
Church of the holy Sepulchre Entrance to the Church

BEETHLEHEM   The church of Nativity

JERUSALEM — Gethsemane General View

CONTENTS